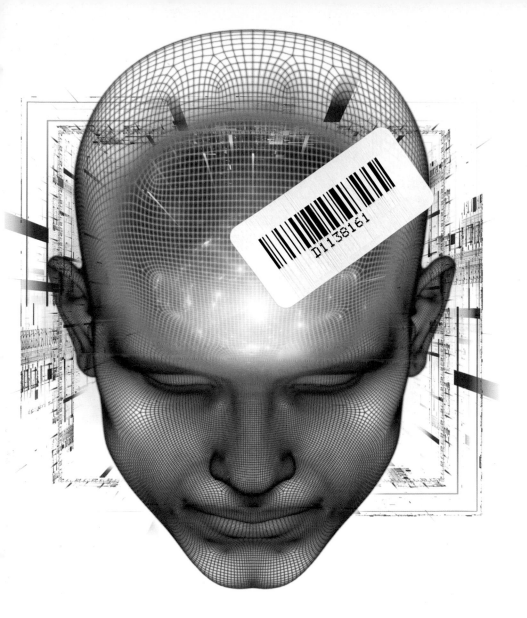

SURVIVAL OF THE SMARTEST

Entrepreneurial strategies for today's college leaders

FIONA HUDSON-KELLY

Survival of the Smartest
Entrepreneurial strategies for today's college leaders
ISBN 978-1-909116-70-2
eISBN 978-1-909116-71-9

Published in 2016 by SRA Books

Printed in Great Britain.

Contents

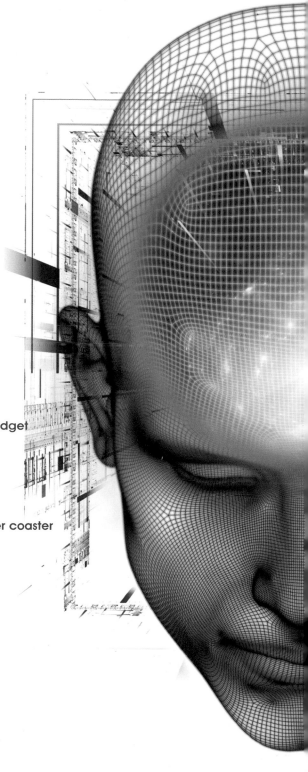

Foreword

Fiona Hudson-Kelly is a lady whom I admire and respect. Over the past five years I have seen Smart Assessor with her at the helm turn into a multi-million pound business. Fiona is someone who has 'been there, done that, read the book, seen the film and got the t-shirt,' so there has never been a better time for this book to be published. It is written in a way that makes it relatable to readers and gives them the inspiration to have a go at the exercises and suggestions in the book.

In case you don't know Fiona Hudson-Kelly's full story, let me tell you what she has achieved in her life so far and how you can expect even more things from her in the future.

At a young age she worked as a commercial apprentice and then retrained as a teacher, leading her to begin helping mothers find their way back into the workplace after having children. Soon, Fiona found her training in demand not only by working mothers, but also by company executives looking for computer skills. She launched – at the age of 26 and after having children of her own – her computer training company, Start-Right, and the company started attracting some big clients such as Pcugoot. This sort of entrepreneurial thinking was practically unheard of at the time, especially for a working mother, and she found the experience rewarding, but challenging. Very soon she was employing 25 people and Start-Right was conducting training courses throughout the country. However, her world would be turned upside down in 2005 when her biggest client at the time, MG Rover, collapsed.

Fiona lost her entire business in just a few days. Her life seemed to crumble after that, but her children kept her motivated, that motivation helping her start a new business, Silver Linings, a year after the collapse. Determination and hard work paid off and she sold the company to take on a new challenge inspired by her son: apprentice programmes. This was the birth of Smart Assessor and Fiona has never looked back since then.

I count myself lucky to know Fiona and regard her as a friend and mentor in my working life. This book is a testimonial to what a person with determination can do. She has worked hard to achieve so much in such a short space of time. This book will give readers the confidence no matter what stage they are in their career to give it a go.

Lindsay McCurdy
CEO of Apprenticeships 4 England

Introduction

As a senior college leader your whole world is changing. Suddenly you're coping with an enormous cultural shift – that of turning into a lean, competitive, entrepreneurial institution which is agile enough to cope with changing demands from both your employer companies and the government.

Budget cuts are nothing new to you, but recent reductions have taken funding uncertainty to a new level. And as if that isn't enough, you're now adjusting to fresh changes to the management of apprenticeships as a whole. What has traditionally been a partnership between your college and the employers has now turned into a buyer/supplier relationship, with you on the selling end and them on the buying. If an employer wants something different from what you've previously offered, it's up to you to provide it or they'll take their business elsewhere. What's more, you've no longer got the monopoly on apprenticeship training provision: employers can also get in on the act.

If you're heading up one of these training provider organisations, you too are going to have to be much more responsive to the demands of your employer companies. They're the ones who will now be making the key decisions about how apprenticeships are run.

So there's political change to your funding, political change to the way in which you deliver apprenticeships and political change to the notion of what a further education college is for. Should there be the same number of colleges as we have now? Maybe we'll end up with fewer, more specialised institutions. Your own college is at this very moment being assessed for fitness for purpose.

Who knows what the future of further education will be?

It's hard, isn't it? How do you turn yourself into this new, entrepreneurial animal, without losing the values you hold so dear? Caring for your students and making sure they receive the best training and education possible has always been your number one priority. And so it should be. But it's not enough now, is it?

This is where I can help. I'm an entrepreneurial business woman (a bit like the kind of person the government wants you to be) who set up my own company, Smart Assessor, especially to help apprentices manage and track their learning. You may already know about us but in case you don't, we're the most innovative online learning and assessing platform around, serving over 200 colleges and training providers along with over 125,000 apprentices. Leading this company has helped me to get familiar with the way you work and the difficulties you have to overcome, so this book is all about helping you to become more businesslike at the same time as enabling you to retain your caring ethos.

Since founding Smart Assessor four years ago, I've built it up from zero to a £2m turnover and have many more ambitious plans ahead. I've done this by being crystal clear on what I want to achieve, ultra-responsive to the needs of my clients, and a persuasive and effective communicator with my potential team. Using technology the right way has also been a vital part of our success; another has been working with the best people to get top results.

We're also an award winning employer of apprentices ourselves, taking the 2013 Small Employer Apprentice of the Year Award for our management of apprentices, so we know what the situation is like from both the employers' and your own perspective. And we've done all this without generous budgets, hundreds of staff or any kind of helping hand. Just like you'll have to do with your own organisation from now on.

So how does this book get you on the right track? It will show you how to create the best mindset for success, where to find the ideas for developing innovative services for your apprentice employers, and the mechanics for launching and marketing a brand new product or service. I'll also be talking you through how to build the support team that's so essential for you to succeed, and help you to find ways of maintaining your momentum over the years to come.

You may not believe you can do this. You may not want to do this. You may not see why you should have to do this. But believe me, you really do need to embrace all these new ways of thinking if your college or training organisation is to survive the next few years, let alone thrive in the decades ahead.

This book is designed to guide you on your journey. It'll be more fun than you think, I promise. And on the way you'll learn all sorts of things about yourself and your work that will underpin your career in the future, wherever it may lie. By the end you'll have a step-by-step plan to turn your institution into an innovative, agile and change-ready organisation, ideally positioned to take advantage of the opportunities ahead. Does that sound good?

The time to start is now. This government isn't going to wait for you to get your affairs in order before it demands you start thinking and working like an entrepreneur. The sooner you begin, the more likely you are to get a head start before the other training providers steal your thunder.

Let's get cracking.

Chapter 1
Start with the end in mind

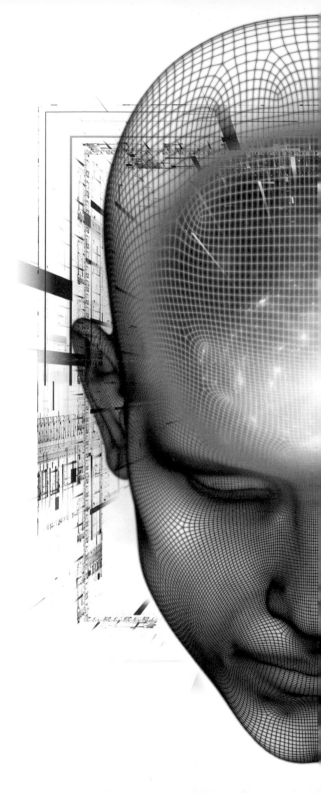

Chapter 1 **Start with the end in mind**

Creating strategic plans will be nothing new to you, but I'm about to show you a fresh, new way of looking at them. It's taking this approach that enabled me to establish Smart Assessor as quickly as I did. I've used all my experience of succeeding and failing in the business world to come up with this way of planning; now you can benefit from what I've learned.

Your end vision is your starting point

Creating your plan with the end in mind is essential. It's all about having purpose. If you don't know your destination, how can you map out your journey? I know that sounds a little corny, but if you can't see, feel and visualise where it is you're going to, how do you know when you've got there, or even if you're on track to arrive?

Many people think of the 'end in mind' as being something that's written on a plan or a wall poster, and of course it can be. But actually it's much more internal than that. It's got to be in your head and heart right from the word go, because if you don't have it embedded deep within you, how can you start to paint a picture of it and communicate it to the people around you?

You have to hold it close, because once you've got your vision everything you do from that point will move you nearer to your goal. And it gives you a laser focus. Distractions around you will try to pull you off track – and let's face it, some of those distractions are quite pleasant and interesting – so your end vision needs to be so compelling you won't allow anything to stop you from making it a reality.

How to create your vision

You'll notice I've not talked yet about how you decide what your actual vision should be (that comes later). This part is all about the mental preparation. You'll also realise this isn't a plan for your audit, financial regulation or OFSTED inspection. You need to have that kind of plan of course, but this is all about your vision. What could your organisation look like in five years' time, and what does that mean for you?

When deciding what you want to achieve, you need to know two things:

• What's worked well, and not so well, for you in the past
• What motivates you to succeed

The first business I set up was an IT training company. Over 15 years I grew it into a solidly successful outfit, only to lose it when our biggest client, the Rover Group, went under. They took us down with them, as they did with many of their other suppliers, and we had to reinvent ourselves and start again.

From that I learned not to put all my eggs in one basket; no company is too big to fail (unless you're a bank, of course).

I'd also set up another business in which I'd gone down the equity finance route. This was great at the beginning, but when I came to sell my share I found being compelled to stay on and manage it didn't give me any personal satisfaction at all. I lost my sense of purpose, which for me is essential for my motivation. I've learned over the years that being in control of my life and business is what gives me my drive to succeed, and by bringing investors into the business I'd lost the ability to be in charge of my own destiny.

So when I set up Smart Assessor I took the learnings from my past experience, and made the decision right from the beginning that not only would I concentrate on gaining a varied client base, but also that I would, in time, sell the business and observe it continue to grow and flourish without me. I knew I needed that crystal clear end goal to keep me focused.

Let's think about you and your 'end in mind'. What do you want to leave behind for others to benefit from? What will be your legacy? Being realistic, with the changes taking place in further education right now, your college may not exist in 30 years' time. You might not see yourself leaving education, and that's fine. But just think, after implementing what you'll learn in this book, you would have the ability to take your experiences to another place with a hierarchical structure and turn that one into a flatter and more agile organisation.

Of course you have regulations to work with, but that doesn't stop you from deciding what you can personally contribute, and how you can deliver your best work. And please don't think you can't tap into your own personal values here, just because it's not your own business. In order to feel energised and focused over a long period of time, your goal needs to matter, *really matter*, personally to you. If you have that, together with a timescale and a challenge that feels realistic and achievable, you can do anything.

When I'm recruiting young people into apprenticeship work in my own company, I tell them, 'You're not going to be here in 10 years, and this job probably won't exist in 10 years. The job for life is long gone, so you need transportable skills to survive.' As a senior manager in your college you owe it to your institution to take the long view.

Yes, but...

Now I know what you're thinking: you get it now – you need to examine your values and decide what you want your college to achieve. But what should you actually *do* in order to create this vision?

There are, of course, many ways of going about this. But I'll help you get started:

1. Decide on what your core, personal values are. I don't mean woolly statements like 'helping our students reach their potential', I mean what really matters to you individually. Examples of values are: independence, love, expression, creativity, communication, security, freedom, authority, realism, order, achievement, autonomy, self-control. The list goes on. Take some time to jot down all the values you feel are essential to you in your life, and when you hit a brick wall, force yourself to carry on some more. Then, narrow them down to the three most important ones; these will be the values that will help to shape your end goal. Why do this? Because if what you want to achieve isn't in tune with your core values, you won't value it highly enough to see it through when times get tough.

2. Work out how much energy you possess to see this through. When I created my timescale for Smart Assessor I worked out how long I could sustain my energy for it, and what would be a realistic timescale for me to sell it in given both my own motivation and the marketplace we operate in.

3. Connect with people who think similarly to you, because there will be so many others around you saying things like, 'What you want to achieve is ridiculous. What are you thinking of? Why on earth do you want to do this?' Nobody can do this on their own, and it's worth bearing in mind that networking is one of the main things entrepreneurs credit with their success. Later on I'll tell you how you can use our Smart Leaders Club for senior education professionals to gather this kind of support around you.

4. Get away from your desk. Have a swim, take the dog for a walk, just get out and really start thinking. What inspires you? Where do you get your inspiration from? This never happens in the office – never, never, never. For instance, I might be sat in a lecture for my MBA course and come up with a brilliant idea that's been prompted by what I've just heard, or it could be as I'm getting out of the shower that inspiration comes. It's certainly not at my desk.

In terms of how you actually create your goal, do what works for you. You'll already have established ways of going about this kind of thing; it may be you're a sticky note lover, or a brainstormer, or possibly you like to get stuck in with a good, old-fashioned spreadsheet. When I first set my vision for Smart Assessor I didn't do any of these things, I just thought about what timescale was realistic for me and figured the rest out from there. But that may not be your style. If drawing a mind map, for instance, is a boost to your creativity, then go for it.

And this isn't something you have to go through alone. You can involve your management team and, even better, people from outside your college. In fact the next chapter will give you some helpful insights on how to use the brains of those around you to make setting your vision a lot easier.

This is a fluid process. My first timescale for exiting Smart Assessor was originally three years after I set it up, but after talking with other serial entrepreneurs, I decided five years was more realistic. It's OK to change your mind.

At this stage you might be saying to yourself, *Well it's all very well for you, you had the freedom to decide your own destiny because you created it from scratch. But here I am, sat in this institution with all the baggage of rules, regulations and past precedents to weigh me down. I've got the government telling me this, I've got employers saying they want that; I've got all these competing demands. I feel like I'm stuck it the middle of it all, so having the freedom to create a vision is a luxury I just can't afford.*

And I sympathise, I really do. But what I'd say is: what is your job then? Are you only managing your organisation, or are you leading it with a true vision that will serve you well into the future?

Entrepreneurs aren't as different as you might think

Did you know most business owners aren't actually entrepreneurs (although some of them might like to think they are)? They either inherited a family business, or went freelance doing something they trained to do in their job. So instead of answering to a boss they can now walk the dog whenever they want, but they don't necessarily earn any more than they did when they were employed.

A true entrepreneur takes risks with their own money in order to create something amazing. Even for them, it's rare to start up a new business and see it zoom straight into the stratosphere. Very few companies experience the phenomenal growth you read about in the press. Smart Assessor's turnover was £2m last year; we're aspiring for £3m this year and £5m next year. When we've hit our £5m turnover we'll have been sustaining 65 per cent growth year on year, which will put us in the top 100 companies in the UK.

But that's not the way it usually goes, and even for successful companies such as mine the growth is kind of messy. If you were to look at it from the outside, you might perceive it as a direct line of growth, whereas in reality it's more like a tangled ball of string eventually leading upwards. Nobody finds it easy.

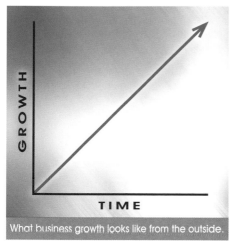

What business growth looks like from the outside.

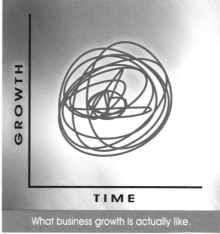

What business growth is actually like.

I'll tell you a secret

The mental shape-shifting you're doing to create your powerful vision – it's hard, isn't it? But if you think you're the only person who feels like that, you're wrong. Nobody likes change, even entrepreneurs who thrive on creating new things.

Did you ever see Steve Jobs wearing anything but jeans and a black polo neck? Have you ever tried to persuade a business person to change their mobile phone or adopt a new way of working? They hate it, and so do I. Take my precious iPhone away from me to replace it with an Android, and I'll freak out!

In this world of constant movement we all need something solid and unchanging to cling onto. What could be your rock? Maybe it's a work system you know serves you well, or a right hand person you trust to support you. You might already have daily rituals or possessions you rely on to keep you grounded.

In some ways it's easier for me as I'm used to a lot of change. I had an unconventional upbringing; when I was young my mum became one of the first students to go to the University of Warwick, and my dad gave up work to look after us kids for a while. This was in the 1960s, so as you can imagine my home was run very differently from those of my friends. Fast forward to the present and I've been a single mum for quite some time, raising my four children on my own. This experience of change and uncertainty being the norm has positioned me differently in life, teaching me that although a support system is crucial, there is only one person you can completely rely on and that's yourself.

In a way, you're in a similar situation. Although you have your management team to help you, the future of your institution is primarily down to you. The easy option is to look for somebody else to fix things, but you know deep down it's your responsibility. And you can do it. Is this the first lot of government changes you've had to deal with? Of course not, and to get to where you are now you'll already have overcome a raft of challenges. What's changing now is your attitude.

What does your vision make you?

You don't have to have all the answers at the beginning, but you do have to have a vision.

For me, my dream was all about creating a really, really successful business that could eventually live without me, and this has a major impact on the decisions I make while I'm running it. Because I know I'm not going to be there forever (just like you're not going to be in your job indefinitely), I have to make sure I'm not the only one who can do everything. This has also meant I've had to confront some emotional issues, such as holding on too long or too hard to things, which is what so many of us do. We identify emotionally with our work, don't we?

If you're a senior manager in your college, that's who you are, right? That's your alter ego. But if you were to give that up in five years' time, having created a hugely successful organisation which is fit for the future, what does that make you then? A principal still? An entrepreneur? A legacy leaver?

This is about saying: what would you like to be?

Chapter 2
Find your gap

Chapter 2 **Find your gap**

You've spent some time looking inwards now, so let's turn our gaze outwards. Your next task is to decide what new products and services you're going to offer your employer companies and your learners. In order to do that you need to figure out what space exists in your marketplace that isn't already being filled by someone else.

You might not have thought of yourself as being in competition in this way before, but now that the marketplace has opened up to new providers of apprenticeship programmes, and colleges of further education are having to prove their worth in a competitive landscape, this is your reality.

What are you really great at that your competition isn't *and* that there's a burning need for in your market? This chapter will show you how to find this out.

Getting out there

So how do you identify that need? You get out more – literally. When was the last time you spent a day in one of your classrooms as a learner? Or when did you most recently spend time with your employer companies, perhaps at a board meeting where you could get to a deep understanding of the issues they face?

You can't come up with a plan in isolation because you run the risk of creating something that could be a dinosaur in ten years' time – and not fit for purpose. With so many disruptive technologies and practices in today's world, things change incredibly fast. You need to have your finger on the pulse in order to know what's really needed (and what's around the corner).

The huge benefit of meeting and talking with your clients, whether they be learners or employers, is that it's a brilliant idea generator. Just picture yourself in one of your employer's board meetings when they start discussing the difficulty of recruiting great young talent. Possibly you could help. You could structure your apprenticeship recruitment procedure so it includes an employer-led assessment, enabling you to hire the right apprentices in the first place.

And if you don't have time to get out and about? Make it. Change your diary around, stop having meetings or find ways to streamline your work. Just do it – it's really not an optional part of your job now.

Don't create a faster horse

One of my favourite quotes is from the car manufacturer Henry Ford: 'If I had asked people what they wanted, they would have said faster horses.' As well as getting out there and listening, you also need to be aware that no one can give you all the answers. You must be that entrepreneur and visionary who does what's right for you *and* your end client.

As I mentioned in the last chapter, at Smart Assessor we have an end goal of getting to £5m in revenue by the end of 2017. Can we do that by doing what we've always done? Probably not, because a lot of the colleges we work with are going to be disrupted by the opening up of the marketplace that I've been talking about so far. So what will we do about it? We'll consult our clients and see what they need. But actually the huge challenge for us is that instead of having a few clients with big contracts, we're probably going to have to sign up many more, smaller contracts. This means we'll need to rethink our business model; we may even have to create a new product for this new market.

So how do we decide what to build? If we were to ask our clients what they want they would probably say, 'More of the same, but a bit better.' Which is all very well, but it's not enough for us because it will mean that:

- What we produce won't be as groundbreaking as it needs to be
- It could go out of date quickly as our competitors start to emulate us (which is a lot easier to do when they're just tweaking something that already exists)

So despite going through a consultation process, it's up to us to visualise what our clients are going to need and want. That's what being a true entrepreneur is, and that's how you dominate your space in the market.

Creating a plan

There are some marketing and business planning tools I'd like to introduce you to here. You may have heard of them already, but you may not have looked at them in the same context as I'm about to share with you now.

PESTLE

Any great product and marketing plan starts with a situational analysis, because you need to know where you are now in order to create a plan for the future. You begin with the world outside your college and then you move inwards to your own organisation.

The PESTLE approach is a great way to begin because it helps you analyse the *external* forces on your college. Each letter stands for a factor which will be influencing what kind of service you offer in the future.

Political

This is largely to do with how the government intervenes in your institution (a big one for you). It can also include new laws and regulations that are due to be introduced. You need to think about how these will affect you.

Economic

The growth or contraction of the economy will have an impact on your funding, together with the public appetite for funding in further education as a whole. Interest rates and taxation policies can also have an effect on your bank balance, and affect what you can afford to implement both now and in the future.

Social

Also known as socio-cultural, these are factors which encompass the shared attitudes and beliefs of your target market (and of the country as a whole). They are also to do with demographics, attitudes to work and careers, and so on. Especially relevant to you, they make a difference to how people view work, learning and apprenticeships from a cultural and social perspective.

Technological

This is self-explanatory, in that we all know what a transformative effect the changes in the technological landscape are having. From your point of view, the use of technology to deliver training no matter where the learner or employer is located is a key issue to consider. You'll also want to think about the investment and savings potentials where technology is concerned.

Legal

Health and safety, equal opportunities, advertising standards, selling laws – you'll be familiar with many of these factors already. For you, areas which affect employee safety and learner privacy will be especially relevant, but also watch out for any new legislation being introduced which will make your work more onerous, or indeed provide an opportunity to give a valued service to an employer.

Environmental

Concerns in this area are, as you know, becoming more and more prevalent. Your employer clients will be striving to carry out their own business in an increasingly environmentally friendly way, and your learners will have grown up with 'green' issues since they were children. There are many challenges and opportunities for you to consider as far as the environment is concerned.

I'd like you to spend some time thinking through each of these six areas, and write down three or four threats and opportunities for each. The threats are relatively easy to identify although the opportunities are less so (you need some lateral thinking with those). They will definitely get you thinking more widely.

The PESTLE factors, although very important for you to take into account, are largely outside your control. Now we'll move inwards to your own organisation and the market you operate within, which is where you can create a more direct impact.

Porter's Five Forces

This well-known marketing tool was developed by the marketing strategy expert Michael Porter, who teaches at the Harvard Business School. It's used by businesses around the world, and is brilliant for helping you to analyse where the power lies in a business situation. Is it with you, with your competitors or is there a gap in the market-place which you could fill?

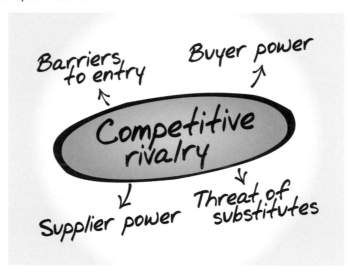

As you can see from this diagram there are five forces which determine whether or not your new offering has the potential to be profitable.

Notes

Supplier power

Here you assess how easy (or otherwise) it would be for your own suppliers to push up their prices. This depends on how many suppliers you have and how easy it would be for you to switch to alternatives. The more you depend on your suppliers, and the harder it would be to change them, the more power they hold. This will have an impact on how profitable you can be.

Buyer power

How easy would it be for your clients to drive your prices down? This is influenced by how important each client is to your business. If you're reliant on a few key clients, you're in a more vulnerable position than if you have a diverse range of clients. Remember, my IT training business went under because I had one large client I was far too dependent on.

Competitive rivalry

How many competitors do you have, and how competent are they? If you have many of them and there isn't much for your clients to choose between you, then there's not a lot stopping your clients from switching away from you to someone else. On the other hand, if you offer something unique and valuable that would be hard for anyone else to provide, the opposite is true.

Threat of substitution

This means how easy (or difficult) it would be for your clients to find a different way of doing what you do. If they could do it themselves, or outsource it easily to someone else, that puts you in a weak position. As a college you've got the potential to offer training services that may be difficult for employers to provide to apprentices, and for learners to source for themselves. But you can't take this for granted.

Threat of new entry

How easy (or difficult) would it be for new further education and training providers to come into your market? If the 'barriers to entry' are low, then new competitors will quickly spring up. If it costs a lot in time and money to set up as a supplier providing what you do, then you're in a more powerful position.

Considering all these factors will help you decide whether, for instance, apprentice-ships are what you're going to go all out for, or if you're going to help your employer organisations in a more holistic way. Note down your thoughts below.

Having done these exercises I'm sure you're still far from deciding exactly what you're going to offer (or if you have, you're probably not sure *how* you're going to do it yet). And that's fine, as in the next chapter I'll be helping you with this. But what you will be doing is making your plans from a position of educated awareness, rather than just using your instinct or assumptions.

Have you started to identify a gap in your market that you could fill more effectively than anyone else? If you have, you're halfway there. Here are some top-of-head ideas for the kind of ideas you might come up with:

• We're going to take 50 per cent of the college online
• After five years I'm going to have a successor in place who I will mentor for the following five years
• 20 per cent of our online students are going to come from overseas
• 50 per cent of our lectures will be delivered by employers
• 10 per cent of our lectures will take place in employers' premises
• We'll team up with a recruitment consultancy to help recruit apprentices

I'm not saying these are right for you, or even what you should go for, because your plans will be influenced by your own vision together with your college's external and internal factors. But one thing's for sure, if you don't come up with your own ideas someone else will fill that gap for you. And soon.

Chapter 3
What's the pain?

Chapter 3 **What's the pain?**

Have a think about the products or services you love using yourself. Each one of them solves a problem or eases a pain. You need to identify the pain your market is suffering from, work out how to anaesthetise it and find out how much your solution is worth to your potential clients. If you don't know what that pain is you can't understand why someone would want to buy from you. And you certainly can't assume they'll carry on using your services any longer, because that's not how your market works now.

Smart Assessor is a system that works for both learners and training organisations. But when we first started it, we built it around the needs of the learners and added in the training providers afterwards. We felt if we designed the system around the teacher or assessor without considering the learner, then it wouldn't have been used enthusiastically; instead, it would have been yet another thing that was done *to* the learner rather than them being at the centre of the journey. You know as well as I do that if a learner isn't engaged and participative, you might be able to drag them through to gaining a qualification but they won't have absorbed all they need to know.

Identifying our market's pain point was made easier by the fact that my own son, who was doing an apprenticeship in fitness training, was struggling to keep up with his coursework because he was so disorganised. By basing our system on his needs we created a baseline for the type of learner we were trying to help, which meant we could make it effective for any kind of apprentice. We asked ourselves: what would somebody like him use, what would he enjoy and what help would he need in getting organised enough to make a success of his apprenticeship? This gave us the idea to include system reminders for visits and to keep the platform intuitive to use. In fact he was part of the inspiration for Smart Assessor in the first place, which just shows how you can get your ideas from anywhere – home, family, friends – as well as work.

If you think about it, you too have competing demands. You're running a college that is putting your learners, quite rightly, at the centre of everything you do. But now you've got to consider the needs of your employer companies and also the government regulators and funders. You have to develop whatever solution you come up with to solve the pain of your market (i.e. the employers), but without neglecting the needs of your students and apprentices. The two go side by side.

The pain, the pain

I'll say this again because it's so important. You won't sell anything to anyone until you've identified these three things:

1. What your potential client's pain is
2. How your solution solves it
3. Whether or not what you're charging for your solution is worth more than the pain they've got

I always make sure my sales people know the answer to these three questions before they go into any sales conversation, and it'll be the same with you when you start promoting your own solution. You may not think of yourself as a sales person, and don't worry about that as I'll be giving you help with that later; just know for now that you need to understand these three elements of market pain.

You have to dig deep to get to the pain. This is because people aren't always open about what keeps them awake at night, or maybe their pain might be disguised as something else. We don't always know what holds us back, do we? How often have you heard the lament from one of your team, for instance, that if they had more resources they could get more done? Then lo and behold, when you give them the resources nothing changes because that wasn't really the problem in the first place – it was something else.

If in pre-internet days I'd asked you how you'd like to book your holiday, you probably wouldn't have suggested an online travel agency because they didn't exist. But when the internet had evolved this would have been a much more obvious solution for you. This is just another way of saying that once someone has taken the first step for you it's much easier to suggest improvements. For instance, everyone hates check-in queues in airports; if you were asked how the process could be improved you might come up with the idea of being able to print your own luggage tag as well as your boarding pass.

The beauty of talking with a range of employers, of course, is you'll spot common challenges and opportunities. If you are sitting in their board meetings, it might not be until the tenth one that you see the common thread between some of the issues raised, but when you spot it you'll know it's a deep pain. Even better, it might be something even the companies themselves haven't identified, so when you present a solution to it they'll be impressed and delighted. They could have a seasonal need for work experience placements, for instance, that your college hadn't previously been aware of. Could you provide an interface whereby the local employers apply to you for students to do short-term project placements, and you supply them for a set period of time?

In order to help both your employer companies and your learners, you need to understand deeply what it feels like to be one of them. For example, by chatting with one of the company directors during a visit, you might pick up on the fact they're worried about a competitor's sexy new tech product that's making them look outdated. Your solution could address that; it might have nothing to do with return on investment, compliance, quality or all the other things you think you sell on – it might simply be helping them with their ego. They're looking for a partner who they can rely on to make it happen easily for them.

Another thing to bear in mind is that once you've identified the true pain point, you might decide to revisit some of the assumptions you made a long time ago. For instance, suppose you had identified a need among your employers for a higher calibre of recruits into apprenticeships, and had decided to build a new process into your service which filters out the wrong candidates. On digging deeper into your employers' needs, though, you now discover it's the employers' management of the apprentices that's the real problem. This could give you the opportunity to offer coaching for employers on how to get the best from apprentices, which you would then add into your portfolio. It could even lead to your college becoming a centre of excellence in this area.

Do you see how this can grow, if you find the real pain?

Here's a step-by-step method for identifying the *right* kind of pain to solve:

1. Identify what you think might be a pain
2. Score it for severity (10 is high)
3. Score it for ease of solution (10 is high). You'll be taking into account Porter's Five Forces in the previous chapter to do this
4. Map these on the chart below. Now you can easily see the pains which score highly on severity and ease of solution – these are the first ones for you to start working on a solution for

Why change is key

As a training provider you're part of the solution for making your employers' businesses great. This is a much more holistic picture than you have probably imagined before. And in order to be open to this, you'll need to change what you're doing and how you're doing it.

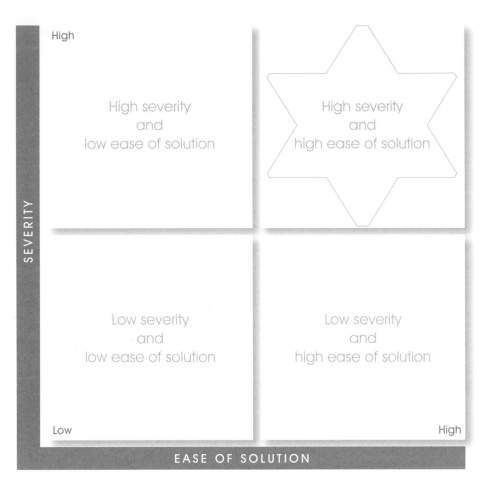

We all know that famous saying about the definition of madness being to do the same thing over and over again, and expect a different result. If you really want your college to succeed, it has to adapt, and in order to do so you've got to change the way you work.

The amazing thing about being open to change is it gives you the opportunity to create things from scratch, and reinvent your market. When I started Smart Assessor there were several competitor products already in existence, one of which was owned by City & Guilds and the other by Pearson, both large international companies. Talk about stiff competition! But by creating a fresh, innovative service from the ground up, we've now gained a 35–40 per cent share of the market.

Of course you can change yourself, but you can't change others. You may have to ride with some of the preconceived views your employer clients have of you. Depending on your existing relationship with them, they may think of you as unengaged with your local business community, and it will take time to turn them around.

This can feel like an uphill struggle, and our online Smart Leaders Club is a safe environment in which to explore some of these challenges with other education leaders in the same boat as you. You won't have all the answers, and nor do I, but it's amazing how together we can help solve each other's problems. You can find it here: www.smartassessor.com

Chapter 4
How to launch in record time

Chapter 4 **How to launch in record time**

In order to be able to give your 16–18 year olds the best facilities and the highest level of learning resources, you'll have to supplement your government funding with commercial revenue. The good news is, in future you'll have fewer regulations to juggle with as the further education marketplace widens out and becomes more innovative. You're actually in a strong position, with the facilities and the relationships you've already got, to be able to leverage those commercial opportunities.

But before I go into how to do this, I'll ask you a question: what's the main thing entrepreneurs do differently from most people, which helps them launch successful new products and services in a short space of time? Would it be raising lots of money, coming up with wacky ideas or using aggressive sales techniques?

The answer is none of the above. Do you want to know the real reason a successful entrepreneur is able to do so much, so quickly? *They don't wait for their new product or service to be perfect before they get it out there.*

This can be an extremely difficult concept for many people to grasp, because we take pride in what we produce. And of course, I'm not suggesting you put anything out there that isn't fit for purpose; your new offering must be capable of delivering what it needs to. But that's the important word: *need*. What does it actually have to be in order to fulfil its basic functions? Should it look lovely, be completely slick and wonderful, and offer every possible option in case someone wants it? The answer is no: all it needs to be initially is innovative and different, and reliable.

If this seems a bit far-fetched, don't worry. In this chapter I'll be taking you through the process of getting a rough prototype of your new product or service into your marketplace, recruiting a small number of trial clients, and using their feedback to create a more sustainable and worthwhile venture than if you'd waited until it was 'ready'.

Why the rush?

Why get it out there in rough form before you perfect it? There are four huge advantages to doing this:

• You'll get in there before your competitors. Apple was one of the first companies to stream music legally and has 'owned' this area for years (remember bricks and mortar retailer HMV who went bust?). Amazon was the first business to sell books online in a major, scalable way, and now they're the market leaders. How would you feel if another college launched the scheme that's currently in your head while you were still agonising over how to perfect it?

- You can learn from the feedback you get from your trial users. These are real world clients with opinions based on their actual usage of your product – there's no theory here. Instead of guessing what people want, you can find out for sure. After all, how else do you know what 'perfection' is?
- You'll be creating a buzz around your product. Having been involved from early on, your trial users will be incredibly loyal and word will spread of its own accord.
- You'll have confidence in your offering. By developing it alongside some trusted partners, you'll know for sure it's what your clients both want and need. This will help you to sell it with confidence; you'll feel convinced it works and will have the case studies to prove it.

Some challenges you'll face

I'll not pretend it's easy to develop things this way, but then if it was, all the other colleges would already be doing it too, wouldn't they? And you don't want to be launching your new service at the same time as them, or heaven forbid, even later. You want to be the first.

So what's stopping you getting it out there before it's perfect? In my experience these are the main reasons.

Resistance from your colleagues

I regularly have big fights with my IT guys at Smart Assessor, because developers always want to perfect their work before they release it. It's in their nature. You may find your teachers and process people are like this as well; it's a battle to get them to realise that what you're launching is good enough for now. They can find it hard to trust that you really will reassess and remodel it from user feedback as time goes by.

One way of approaching this is to give them examples of other products that have succeeded because they were one of the first in the marketplace and were then refined over time, particularly outside the world of education. A great example is Starbucks. In the beginning Starbucks was a coffee bean and equipment retailer, not a cafe. Their then retail director, Howard Schultz, was in Milan for a trade show when he noticed how popular the coffee shops were, each one crammed with customers enjoying their espressos, cappuccinos and the sense of community on offer. Enthused by this, on his return to the US he tried to persuade Starbucks' owners to open a cafe to see if it would work at home. They refused but eventually agreed to him setting up a trial espresso bar in one of their new coffee bean outlets in Seattle. It was an instant success, bringing in hundreds of customers every day. And I think we all know how the rest of the story goes.

Can you recognise the key elements of this from what I've been saying? Schultz had an innovative idea (by getting out and about – see Chapter 2), he set up an imperfect trial to test the concept and through feedback was able to develop it into the enormously successful business it is today. Yes, you might have your opinions about the dominance of Starbucks on our high streets, but the point is that this is an exceptionally successful business. Even the big start small.

Your own internal resistance

Depending on your own personality, you may find yourself baulking at the idea of putting something out there that isn't perfected. And that's understandable – you haven't got to being a leader in your field by being slapdash and amateur, after all. But that's not what I'm talking about. Your product or service needs to be great; it just doesn't need to be completely finished.

If you think about it, launching something that isn't 'perfect' in every way demands you put your ego to one side. You're saying to the world, 'I believe in this thing. I know it's good, but I need to know what I should change in order to make it better. And I'm asking you to help me.'

It also entails being OK with the idea of 'failing'. After all, you teach your students to pass, not fail, don't you? In an educational setting this can lead to many people being quick to point to initiatives that didn't work in the past, and using them as a reason not to try something new in the future. But most new projects will 'fail' to a certain extent, in that they're never 100 per cent right from day one. The trick is to get early feedback and be resilient enough to pick up the pieces, improve and move on. Losing money in one area doesn't mean you can't make it back several times over in another.

It's really a mindset shift, and it's one you need to make if you want to move forward successfully.

Your own attitude to risk

If you've ever been to see a financial adviser, you'll know they usually do a risk profile on you by asking questions to gauge your attitude to risk. At the end you'll get a number which denotes the way you feel about it; for instance, a seven out of ten would mean you're pretty comfortable with taking financial risks.

How do you think you would score? And just as interestingly, how would your team fare in a test? Ideally you'd want a spread of attitudes to risk. A whole team of extreme risk takers would make for a rocky ride, whereas a team comprised of risk averse people would move much too slowly.

Take the risk profile test

You could try out this test on yourself and your team – it's a great way of working out who's going to be most and least enthusiastic about new ideas. For each question, give yourself a score of 1 to 5, with 1 being completely disagree and 5 being completely agree.

1. Whenever I make plans, I enjoy thinking they could change at the last minute.
2. My friends think of me as a wild and exciting person.
3. Rules are meant to be broken.
4. I'm always happy to take a risk if there's something in it for me.
5. I love amusement parks with crazy rides.
6. Whenever I submit a written report, I don't worry about checking it for errors.
7. Before taking a big decision, I listen to my instinct rather than doing research.
8. Looking back, I can see plenty of times when my actions were more risky than I thought at the time.
9. I can't stand repetitive tasks at work.
10. I find it exciting to work on a project that could fail.

If you scored 1–19: you are very risk averse.

If you scored 20–34: you've got a balanced attitude to risk.

If you scored 35–50: you've got a very adventurous attitude to risk.

Which are you? How does your team stack up in terms of attitude to risk? When you're launching a new venture you could make best use of your 'risky' people by getting them involved early; they'll be comfortable with taking a chance. Your team members who find risk taking more difficult are best focusing on improvements and ongoing management of the project.

How we launched Smart Assessor

It can be helpful to see how another small business has done the same thing as I'm advising you to do, and there's no business I know better than my own. We've made a big splash in a small pond with our online platform, and we did it by getting our system out there long before it was perfect (it never is, by the way).

I've already talked about how we used my son's difficulties with organising his learning to develop the software that Smart Assessor is based on. When it came to the moment at which we were confident the basic system worked, we decided not to launch it to all the colleges from the word go. Instead, we presented it to a select group of small training provider companies. Why did we choose them? For a start, being independent businesses, we knew they would be more likely to take a chance on us than the large colleges. And second, because they were smaller, they were more agile and adaptable; we could talk to the main decision makers quite easily without wading through layers of management and gatekeepers.

In order to show the system at its best we set up a series of launch events around the country. When I say 'launch events' don't imagine glitzy halls; they were just hotel function rooms in which we put on a working lunch and demonstrated our system to the training providers we'd invited to attend. We'd got their contact details from an online database and had called them up and emailed them, explaining the benefits of attending our event: namely the opportunity to try out a fresh and different way of helping students track their learning, with a tasty lunch thrown in.

We knew we were looking for around a dozen partners, or 'trailblazers' as we called them, of different sizes and from a variety of sectors, and this we achieved. They bought into our system partly because they were excited by the prospect of being able to shape the end product, and also because they got it for a discounted price in return for feedback. And before you worry about offering financial incentives, it's worth noting we still made £98,000 in revenue in our first year.

Because we only had a small number of trailblazers we were able to have a very open dialogue with them. We didn't have a formal feedback process; instead we focused on spending time with them, learning what was working and what needed to change, and also what we should develop from scratch. If you recall, when I talked earlier in the book about getting into your clients' meetings to discover what they really think, that's what we did – we got out there and listened. I even remember going to a nursery to watch the first batch of learners (nursery nurse trainees) being shown how to use Smart Assessor. It was fascinating to be a fly on the wall, listening not only to their gripes but also to what they loved about it. This early adopter is now one of our biggest clients.

I hope you can see from this how relatively easy it is to launch and get feedback. It doesn't have to involve endless paperwork, it can just be a matter of common sense. Thinking about how to recruit your own trailblazers is all about putting yourself in their shoes, and then building the personal relationships to make it happen. Pick up the phone, go and see them, and just do it but never give anything away for free as it wont be valued.

As a footnote to this, it's worth mentioning another way in which we weren't 'perfect'. We knew our core market for Smart Assessor would be large colleges, training providers and employers. But we also knew we'd be unlikely to recruit many trailblazers from them, for the reasons I've given above. So our triallers weren't in our exact target market, but we figured that was OK because given our own team only comprised of four people at that time, we needed the process to be flat and easy. And it worked out fine. In fact, we still have a great relationship with all of our early users; one is a tiny training provider, buying only four licences a year not in our target market. But because it's her, we make an exception and respect her loyalty.

Why did we launch quick and small?

Because it was the best way to deliver something we knew people actually wanted, rather than what we *thought* they wanted. When you're creating something really new, even your potential clients might not necessarily be able to envisage what they desire, but once you've broken the mould in terms of a concept, the refinements should come from the client.

We knew that for our college clients, quality assurance was going to be a key part of the system. But we didn't build it into the initial product because we thought it would be interesting to find out how our trailblazers would like it to work if it wasn't 'technology'. We asked them what was happening well and badly for them in the 'real world', and then made it work with our online system. That way, rather than giving them something that was technologically slick but didn't fit with their current working practices, we took the best of what they were already doing and put that online.

Another example of how we improved our product through feedback was when some of our trailblazers told us they were frustrated they could only use it when they had access to the internet. So we created a downloadable programme which worked offline on their laptop and synchronised when they got back onto Wi-Fi.

I'll be honest, sometimes we got feedback we didn't want to hear. Did we jump at the chance of investing resources in this offline version when it wasn't something we'd factored in at the beginning? Not at first, but after we'd had the same comments from a variety of people we knew we had to listen and act.

What you can take from this

If you think about it, you've already got focus groups and trailblazers all around you: your students and your employer companies. Is your relationship with these companies such that you could go deep into their business, talk to them about their supply chain and identify areas where you could pick up new projects? Just suppose you've done some work with a major car manufacturer in your area. You could ask them if there are opportunities for you to collaborate with their other suppliers – anything from components manufacturers to stationery. Could they also be your clients? And could you replicate what you're doing for your main client right the way down through their supply chain?

You'll never know unless you visit them and ask. If you feel like 'sales' is a dirty word, think of it this way: by not asking what else you could help with, you're doing them a disservice. You really are of benefit to them when you find out what they need and give it to them.

Like with Smart Assessor, your biggest clients aren't necessarily the ideal ones for your trailblazers. Large organisations don't usually adapt well to things not going smoothly with a new product, and prefer a sure bet which is low risk. We mitigated this by working with clients who had hundreds of learners rather than thousands, so when we were implementing all the changes that came out of the pilot phase we could manage it fairly easily. Another way of approaching this is to work with a larger client but in a limited part of their business. For instance, we collaborated with two larger colleges, but instead of going college-wide with them we kept our trial to two or three small curriculum areas.

I hope this has fired you up to get your ideas out there before they're perfected. It really is the key to your success.

Chapter 5
Clever marketing on a
tight budget

Chapter 5 **Clever marketing on a tight budget**

You'll probably not find this surprising by now, but I'm going to bust another business myth for you. You may have assumed that start-up companies have huge marketing budgets – the kind you couldn't possibly match. And you would be so wrong. With a team of only four people and a few thousand pounds to spend on promotion at launch, we had to work really hard at marketing Smart Assessor, and yet we still managed to generate a good amount of noise in our marketplace.

There are four key steps to creating a successful, low budget marketing campaign:

1. Knowing exactly who you want to talk to (and I mean exactly)
2. Finding out where their 'watering holes' are (where they hang out)
3. Creating an innovative marketing communications plan which speaks clearly to them
4. Carrying out the plan and reviewing it

I'll come clean here and say I have a marketing background, which made the marketing element of promoting Smart Assessor easier for me than it would have been for many people. But that's all to your benefit, because I'm about to reveal to you some incredibly effective, low-cost marketing techniques that you can use not only for launching your new product or service, but for marketing it long term as well.

First things first

You've created a pilot version of your new product or service, you've had feedback from your trailblazers, and now you've developed a more finessed version that you are happy to launch into your marketplace. What's the next thing you need to do?

You have to get crystal clear on who you want to 'talk' to with your marketing, and *narrow your audience down* as much as possible. I can't stress enough how important this is for a cost-effective campaign, and I'll explain more by using us as an example.

We knew from the word go our product was for apprentices only, not for full-time students, university students or any other kind of learner. Not because the latter groups wouldn't find it useful – on the contrary, many might have benefited from it – but because they were not in our target market.

I know what you're thinking. Limiting your audience can feel incredibly uncomfortable, even counter-intuitive; you want to sell to as many people as possible, so why not promote it as broadly as you can? Because this will result in fewer profitable sales, not more. I'll explain why below.

You're not a multinational company

Huge organisations (the household names) can afford to target broad audiences with their marketing, because they have the budgets to match. And this actually fits with their business model, because their success is usually based on having economies of scale; they need to sell lots and lots of products in order to make a profit.

Even if you head up a large college, in the general scheme of things it's still a relatively small business. You're one of many colleges in England, and your activities are restricted to a certain extent by your physical location. So the marketing budget you have per potential client is pretty small, and you need to focus your spend very carefully in order to make it work hard for you.

Credibility

When you're a new player in a market, you have to establish your credibility and expertise very quickly. It's a lot easier to do this when you're only marketing to a small, core audience who you know you can serve extremely well.

You'll remember we developed Smart Assessor using my experience of my son's difficulties with organising his apprentice learning. This meant we knew the system would be perfect for apprentices. We also knew it might work for other learners, but we weren't completely sure and couldn't prove it. If we had gone into the university market, for example, we wouldn't have had the real world examples and experience to back up what we were offering.

Another aspect to this is that by starting small you'll not run the risk of creating a demand that's too big, too soon. What if you were to launch full scale and then not be able to satisfy all your new clients? You need to make sure you've got the resources in place to provide an excellent service; your market won't give you a second chance.

Ease of access and communication

Another reason we decided to focus on the apprenticeship market was that the apprenticeship funding rates for colleges were often higher than for full-time students. Also, in colleges, apprenticeships tend to be managed separately from other students, which means they're already using their own technology solutions. This created an easier environment for us to sell within.

This relative independence in the apprenticeship culture means the college decision making process is more streamlined, which in turn means it's simpler for us to communicate with them than it is with the college as a whole. Being able to access and talk to your target market without having to go through layers of management is a huge bonus when you're creating a marketing campaign.

By the way, even though we're now well established as a business, we still haven't gone into the full-time student market on our own. Instead we're partnering with an expert in this area to sell our product through them. We know where our strengths lie, and we stick to them.

It helps you to spread the word

When you're a big fish in a small pond word spreads quickly, especially if you're operating in a market in which you have a high degree of credibility and expertise. You become trusted as the go-to expert, whereas if you try to spread yourself too thinly you risk becoming a jack of all trades in the public eye. Alongside this, when your target market is too diverse you're not able to serve it so well, which makes you vulnerable to larger competitors who are able to show expertise to *their* markets.

As you can see, your choice of target market is a crucial one. It needs to be tightly focused on a readily defined group, which is:

- Small enough for you to spend money on in a meaningful way
- Within your core area of expertise (for the product or service you're promoting)
- Relatively easy to access and talk to
- Profitable enough to be worth it

How to pick your focused audience and find their 'watering holes'

You've probably already come up with some ideas about who you could target, but now you need to get specific. Which employers do you already have good relationships with, who might be receptive to your new offering? What do they have in common with each other? Is it the subject area for your learners or the sector the employers are in, for instance? And what's different about them that you can leverage elsewhere? For instance, you might be brilliant with hairdressers and have developed a niche service of helping small salons with their business planning; you'll want to find more salon owners so you can introduce your service to them.

Let's run with this example. The first thing you would need to do is find out where those small salon owners hang out, either physically in the 'real world' or online; these spaces are their 'watering holes'. To start this process, think about the characteristics of a small salon owner. What are they like? Are they male or female? What age might they be? What interests do they have both in and outside work? Are they likely to go to local community events, professional events or both? In their case not only do they have physical premises you can identify, but they will also go to product launches and hair shows. Online, are there LinkedIn and Facebook groups for salon owners that you could participate in? Remember the pain points in Chapter 3 – hairdressers will have their own problems, and will gather together to help each other solve them.

The beauty of identifying and reaching these watering holes is that you've already done part of your marketing work; someone else has set up the group or event, and all you have to do is turn up in a helpful way. You'll soon find a ripple effect taking place as well. Once you've found one watering hole, that tends to lead to another and another, and so on. You're not going to know them all at the beginning, so just make a start.

Can you or your team picture yourselves hanging out with hairdressers? Possibly not! If you're like most college principals you'll probably prefer chatting with others in the same field as you. But tapping into the world of your core clients is actually what this whole book is about – getting to know them, helping them in a knowledgeable way and then selling to them as a result.

Or you could spend £10,000 on advertising with far less effective results. It's up to you.

It's time to get clever

A limited marketing budget used in the right way is a bit like setting off a firework – small but incredibly effective.

Staying with our salon owners' example, just suppose you were to take a stand at, or sponsor, a hair show. In your 'old' marketing mindset you would probably book the stand, stick up some posters, install your staff and wait for people to visit you. And wait. And wait. And then write the whole thing off as a waste of time.

Why wouldn't it have worked? Because people don't go to shows to visit the stands, they go to take part in the learning events and catch up with their colleagues and friends. So you've got to be really innovative if you want to talk to the right people.

Here's what you could do instead. Find out in advance who's going to the show (it's very easy, just look on the conference website) and decide on a small subsection of them to target. For instance, the event may be in London but you're based in Birmingham, so you could identify 45 salon owners who come from your area. Then you need to give these people (and *only* these people) a reason to come and talk to you at your stand; maybe they could collect a sample, or have a bespoke one-to-one chat about how business planning improves the success rate of salons in Birmingham. I can guarantee you nobody else at that event will do this, so you'll be head and shoulders above your competition (if you'll forgive the pun).

Here's what we've done in the past. For our stand at the AoC Conference (an annual conference where senior leaders in further education can discover, learn, celebrate and shape the future together) this year, we recognised that the only reason there are always stands at events is because they make money for the exhibition management, not because hordes of delegates actually want to visit them. As I mentioned above, they'd much rather attend the seminars and chat with their contacts and friends. In the very small amount of time remaining, they might decide to visit the odd stand, and we wanted to make sure ours was the one they chose to come and see. So we created a list of our existing clients ahead of time and sent out a fun voucher with a PIN code to win a small prize. Our clients had to visit the stand to see if they had won. In fact we sent out a series of mail-outs, so they didn't just get it once but several times. And they loved it. We got the chance to talk to them about Smart Assessor, get valuable feedback and identify upsell opportunities. Nurturing your existing clients is too often overlooked, yet it is much easier to sell added value to people who already trust you.

Of course, other people visited our stand too, especially when they saw there was something interesting going on which gave us the opportunity to introduce our existing clients to prospects who hadn't used Smart Assessor. We were ruthlessly efficient in our selection and targeting of the people most important to us, our loyal customers.

How to generate clever marketing ideas

So you understand what needs to be done, and now it's just a question of doing it. How do you generate ideas for clever marketing campaigns that target a tightly focused audience in a way that stretches a small budget to its utmost?

There are many ways you can approach your market. It could be via events (either those you attend or those you organise yourself), direct mail, email, thought leadership marketing (that's when you set yourself up as an expert in the media), low cost advertising, social media, physical networking – the list is endless. It all comes down to where the watering holes are. Take the example of participating in a LinkedIn group for salon managers; if your expertise is in helping them create strategies and business plans, you could write blog posts on these topics and upload them to the group, starting conversations which demonstrate your expertise.

This will involve you finding and using the skills and knowledge you already have within your college, which is something you might not have done before. Your business studies department could contribute content and ideas, for instance. Or how about asking the people hanging around the watering holes what they want, and what their problems are? This will spark ideas aplenty.

We considered setting up our own online social media platform for apprentices via the Smart Assessor system, and then we thought, 'Hang on a minute, Facebook's got 1.5 billion users, why not tap into that?' In the end, as our apprentices don't actually buy the product themselves, we've set up a LinkedIn group for colleges and training providers which has been very effective at helping both them and us. Our Smart Leaders Club for senior college leaders is even better at helping them to interact and advise each other, with lots of virtual events to enable them to learn about being an entrepreneurial educator – find out more here: www.smartassessor.com

Use your point of difference

Once you've figured out your target audience and their watering holes, the next aspect you need to get clear on is what makes your product or service different and special – and then hammer home the message consistently. For instance, we've put the line 'Audit Ready Every Day' on all our marketing material, because we know that's one of the things that makes us unique and our clients really value. Our system allows all the key performance indicators (KPIs) to be visible at a glance, which means if tomorrow any of our clients were to get an inspection, they'd be prepared. Of course, your point of difference needs to relate to the pain you're easing for your target market. What would it be?

Creating your marketing campaign

Now you know what you're wanting to achieve with your marketing and who you're aiming at, how do you create your campaign? This can take many different forms, but they all follow the same steps:

1. Identify your tightly focused market
2. Find their watering holes
3. Decide what you can do most effectively with your budget
4. Come up with fresh ways of approaching your market, using your point of difference
5. List out the different platforms you can use (event, email campaign, etc.) Never use just one method, always try a combination so you can create more of an impact
6. Carry out the marketing
7. Analyse afterwards what worked and what didn't
8. Use this knowledge to define exactly where your most profitable clients are coming from, and target others like them

You'll need to map out your planned campaigns over the year, taking the watering holes as your inspiration for timing. So if there's a big show or seasonal event coming up you can tap into that, as well as carrying out your regular marketing activity.

Here's an example plan to help you to get started. You'll need to expand it to include your dates as well. (See the diagram on the next two pages.)

When you're doing your post-campaign analysis, don't rely on instinct or memory for things that have worked well. It's funny, even though I'm a marketer by background, I'm realising as I'm writing this book that I've fallen into the habit of forgetting to question this. Recently we did a review of all our marketing over the past year, and the most successful of everything was a single direct mail campaign. This contained a cranberry-flavoured teabag along with our new brochure, which explained how to be audit compliant. The message in the accompanying letter went along the lines of, 'You'll be especially interested in page five. Why don't you make yourself a cup of tea and then get in touch if you think we can help you?' Being honest, if I'd relied on memory alone I would never have credited this campaign as being our most successful, but the figures proved otherwise.

I hope you feel confident by this point that whatever your budget, you can still market effectively as long as you're laser focused and innovative about it. The small, clever player is always the winner of the marketing budget effectiveness award.

Smart Strategic Marketing Plan

	January	February	March	April	May
Blog	▶ · · · · · ·	· · · · · · ·	· · · · · · ·	· · · · · · ·	· · · ·
LinkedIn	▶ · · · · · ·	· · · · · · ·	· · · · · · ·	· · · · · · ·	· · · ·
Twitter	▶····················	··············	··················	···········	·········
Email with call to action	▶ · · · · ·	· · · · · · ·	· · · · · · ·	· · · · · ·	· · · ·
Direct mail			▶ · · · ●		▶ · ·
SMS – text messages	▶ · · · · ·	· · · · · · ·	· · · · · · ·	· · · · · ·	· · · ·
PR – professional journals		▶ · · · ●			▶ · ·
Referral marketing (WOM)	▶ · · · · ·	· · · · · · ·	· · · · · · ·	· · · · · ·	· · · ·
Speaking opportunities		▶ · · · ●			▶ · ·
Ask the experts webinars			▶ · · · · ·	· · · · · ·	· · · ·
Case studies				▶ · · · · ·	· · · ·
Hosted events	▶ · · · ●			▶ · · · ●	

Key Message: You are in safe hands with us

June	July	August	September	October	November	December

Start and end points

▶······● Daily
▶·····● Weekly
▶····● Monthly
▶···● Quarterly

Chapter 6
Building your dream team

Chapter 6 **Building your dream team**

Just as a huge marketing budget isn't essential for creating an effective marketing campaign, so you don't need a vast, sprawling team to launch and manage an innovative new product or service. I'm sure you're well used to working with restricted resources to achieve outstanding results, so you don't need advice from me on how to do that. But what I think you'll find inspiring is how much I and my team have managed to get done, despite there being only four of us at the start of Smart Assessor.

You'll also need to bear in mind that in your new, entrepreneurial world, you're probably not going to be looking for candidates in your standard 'pool' – your projects will demand fresh talent from different areas. So the old way won't work for you anymore. Instead of bringing in a college lecturer with their standard qualifications and experiences, you're going to be seeking out people with a whole range of difference backgrounds. The problem is, you might not be sure how to find and recruit these special people, which is what I'm going to help you with here.

Trust your instincts

Whenever I recruit anybody, I place a lot of faith in my instincts. This can be hard in a public sector environment in which form filling is as much a part of recruitment as intuition, but if you ignore that niggling voice telling you there's something wrong, you'll live to regret it. Your intuition is usually right. Trust it.

Of course, being legally compliant in your recruitment and selection is a given, both to avoid getting into trouble and because it's the right thing to do. In fact it should be in all sectors, not just the public. But once you've dealt with that, could there be something telling you the person you're interviewing isn't the right one for you? Alternatively might someone else be the best candidate, despite what it says on paper?

I often think we have two personalities at work: one when everything's going smoothly and one when there's a crisis. At the time when I created my senior team at Smart Assessor I approached people I'd already worked with in some way, or who came through a network I was familiar with. So I'd had the opportunity of seeing them in different situations – the good, the bad and the ugly. This gave me a privileged position in terms of predicting how they would perform in any circumstance.

You won't necessarily have the opportunity to experience your candidates first hand like this, but your networks are still a valuable source of feedback. You can ask for written references, but what do they really tell you? Why not put the six degrees of separation rule into practice and ask around for people, who know people, who know your candidates? What are they really like? How well do they cope when things go wrong? How inspiring are they to work with? Remember networks aren't always physical; online social platforms like LinkedIn can be a big help when you're wanting to find out who knows who.

Next, how do you unpick someone's personality when you're interviewing them for a job? We favour scenario interviews for everybody who joins us, no matter how junior. We give them an imaginary situation in advance (based on our own experience) and ask them to prepare a presentation explaining what they'd do. It gives us the chance to see them in action so much more vividly than if we had done a straightforward interview. We also use assessment centres, where we watch all our candidates (even the younger graduates) do a whole day's worth of activities dealing with a series of scenarios on the spot. Through this we see how they interact with others, make use of their own resources and deal with difficulties. And this is really when the intuition comes in; I get a feel for their personality when I see how they talk and listen, or whether they participate in a helpful way. For instance, if I'm looking for somebody with strong leadership qualities I'd want to get a feel for their ability to inspire and direct others.

Now I know what you're thinking: *I haven't got time for this!* And neither do I. But I know if I get this bit wrong, especially for a senior team member, the consequences will be catastrophic. I think of it like a personal relationship. Would I rush into a marriage just because the guy looked good on paper, even though my instincts didn't connect with him?

You'll have recruited many, many people in your time. It's worth reflecting on when it's worked well and when it hasn't. Did you have an intuition at the time which told you how the person was going to turn out? Your gut feelings are probably stronger than you think. And trusting your instincts doesn't stop once you've done the interview, either. If you come to sense your new recruit is really not the right person you have to act quickly, even if it's only two or three weeks after they've started. You must go with that concern.

Your dream team

By now you'll be getting the picture that this isn't about the numbers in your team, it's about having the right types of people around you, both in terms of personality and skills. Developing, launching and managing your new venture is a long, hard road, so surrounding yourself with people who want the same things out of it as you do is vital. Your new team has to be the one that knows how to get back on track when a curve ball hits them, will work the weekend when needed, and will be enthusiastic and focused most of the time. They're the ones who will help you to achieve the vision you set at the beginning so, although it sounds a bit corny, if you get it right they really will be your dream team.

When I started forming my team, the one person I brought on board who I hadn't worked with previously came from a very different background to me. That appointment brought a whole different dynamic to our business; she helped us to develop a much keener sense of urgency, which was fantastic. I'd say having a variety of life experience and education within your team is a great way of helping everyone to question everything. This woman challenged so much of what we took for granted. We'd thought the way we did things was the only way, but she helped us to see there were better methods.

In fact I originally met her when she did a presentation to a women's networking group I belong to called Scary Women (taking my own advice, I was getting out and about in my business community). You may or may not decide to attend local networking events, but if you're sitting in one of your employers' board meetings as a way of getting to know their pain points and identify someone there who could help you, why not suggest they take on a placement working with you? After all, if your end game is to create something that employers really want, who better to be part of your team than someone who's living that every day?

So we know we want a fantastic team and we understand it's down to using our intuition. What else do we need to know?

It's the who, not the how many, that matters

A dream team is about quality not quantity. Initially you're probably looking for a team of three or four people, because if you go for anything larger you'll get drawn into endless meetings and talking. You want to trust that core team to deliver in their areas of expertise, and you need them to feel as invigorated, enthused and motivated as you are. You can't do that and be spreading yourself too thinly at the same time.

Remember that although you're technically the boss, you're not the most important person. The best people to have in your team are those who are better at what they do than you are; how else can you leave them to get on with it?

Choose widely and wisely

I'm sure you know what you're great at and what you're terrible at. The thing is, you haven't got the time to change the last lot, so you need complementary skills in your team. Let's face it, technical skills are easy to get hold of. What I'm really talking about here is recruiting people with innate qualities that are different from your own.

How do you know how to complement yourself? By having enough self-awareness to understand where your strengths and weaknesses lie. Most of us go through life without having any real depth of understanding about ourselves, or maybe we think we do, but it's not accurate. So how do you go about getting that knowledge? For myself, I've had counselling training which has been a great way of examining my behaviours and motivations in-depth. I've also gone through, as I'm sure you have, copious leadership programmes in which I've taken part in personality profiling and 360 degree feedback. So the tools to help us develop self-awareness are all around.

Maybe you could dig out your notes from the last management training you went on; how could you use them to understand yourself more fully? Or ask people what you're like, not just at work but outside it too. Kids, siblings and other relatives are good for this; you want to ask people who'll tell you the unvarnished truth. I get told I interrupt a lot and can be abrupt, but then I also get feedback that I'm great at getting things done. And because I know I'm not so strong in the 'touchy-feely' area, I need someone on my team who's good at pouring oil on troubled waters.

The key thing is to listen. How often do we hear the same thing over and over again, but ignore it? This is about acknowledging your weaknesses and being OK with them. As I said before, you don't have time to change them so just compensate for them within your team. If you have a tendency to jump straight into things without think-ing, for instance, then you'll want a more risk averse team member to balance you out. People are a bit like a box of Liquorice Allsorts – a whole mixed bag of different personality types.

That's not to say there aren't certain traits you want *everyone* in your team to have. A can-do attitude and the ability to stay laser focused are essential. We all know how hard it can be to wake up some mornings and feel enthusiastic about our day ahead; I imagine even a top athlete like Mo Farah starts some days feeling a bit achy and despondent if he's lost a race. So nurturing your motivation is important, and one of the best ways of doing that is to be with other people with the same hunger to get things done as you have.

Another thing to ask yourself is, do you actually want to enjoy the journey? I hope so. When something comes along to blindside you, a fun culture in your team means you're able to recover from it by laughing at yourselves or the situation. One afternoon a month we have a team building day with a light-hearted theme which everyone can enjoy. Which leads nicely into the next element of building a dream team…

Building a close and trusting working relationship

A great team is almost like a family; you become as close to each other as you are to your brothers and sisters. This results in the odd squabble of course, but also the ability to be yourself. You should feel comfortable just blurting out what you think or feel – it might not always be particularly tactful or politically correct, but having an underlying mutual respect means you can express yourself without any repercussions. It's a huge relief.

Bonding is also helped by having a shared sense of your journey together. As I mentioned at the beginning, I have always planned to exit my business within the next few years, and my whole team knows that. In fact they are all shareholders, so when we sell the business they'll be financially remunerated by that as well. One of my team will step up as chief executive officer (CEO), and she's preparing for that right now.

With your family team, you don't have to put on a suit to gain respect, you just have to be you. When you think about it, you probably spend more time with these people than with your real family, so it makes sense to have a close and supportive relationship. And the key to all of this is trust. My team members feel fine with having a meltdown in front of me, because they know I'm there to support them just as they're there to support me.

How to attract the best people

High quality people can choose where they work, so you need to inspire them to come to you. Part of this is about including them on your journey, as I explained above. If your outcome is the same as their outcome, there's a good fit between you.

However, if you're anything like me you won't have a budget for six figure salaries, so a little creativity with how you attract the best people goes a long way. One method is through performance-related pay. High performers are always happy to be paid based on their achievements; they have confidence in their ability to do well and are prepared to work hard enough to make their promises a reality. And with that performance comes the success of your venture.

There's really no ceiling on what you can achieve in this way, and that doesn't just go for senior managers. Every single one of our employees has a bonus based on their own personal KPIs; even the most junior of roles attracts a 10 per cent performance-related bonus. This bonus isn't just based on their own work but also on the success of the business, so if we exceed our targets everyone gets rewarded. That's a really, really effective way to motivate people.

I'll give you an example. At four o'clock one Friday afternoon we sent out a mailshot to 250 people; we hadn't planned for it to be a 'snail mail' campaign, it was supposed to be an e-shot, but we decided at the last moment that a mailshot would be more effective. So we did a good old-fashioned mail merge, printed off the letters, matched them with the envelopes and all started out well. But then we realised something had gone horribly wrong. It turned out the envelopes were the wrong format, which meant the addresses on the letters wouldn't show through unless we re-folded the paper for each one individually. The thing was, we'd already started packaging some of them, so the letters and envelopes were out of sync – what a nightmare! And do you know what? Everybody (and I mean everybody) stayed – not just the sales team who were responsible, but all our staff, until it was done. We had a few beers and everyone had a laugh about it, but we stayed to get it finished because that's the culture we have. The success of the business is everyone's success.

Your team could look like anything

If you've been working in the education sector for a while, you probably think of an employee as being someone who comes to your offices from Monday to Friday (or maybe part-time). That's what they do, right? At Smart Assessor we have to attract, and retain the most talented developers in the UK. These people can choose who they work for and are in very high demand. But if you want to recruit the skills and personalities that are absolutely right for your venture, be open-minded about the way in which you expect them to work. It might mean them operating from home, or even in a different part of the country. A well-performing team can come in all sorts of different, unexpected shapes and sizes.

We live in a global village now. In fact in my company we outsource to two different countries and operate in a third (and we're pretty tiny in the worldwide business stakes!) Australia, America and India – three different time zones and some of them I've never even been to. Part of the entrepreneurial mindset is not accepting that the norm has to be the norm any more.

How about taking on a contractor just for a specific project? Or paying someone by results instead of a salary? Could you liaise with a self-employed assistant online? There are numerous possibilities for creating a varied and exciting team.

Some things about teams I'm deliberately not telling you

In a chapter about building your dream team you might have expected me to talk about key functions, HR policies, job specifications and so on. And I've not done that, partly because you know it already, but also because it's not the point. What really matters is creating and communicating a journey that you can all be on together, with people who make things happen.

As you know by now, I've always been a bit odd. From having a mum who went to university when I was three, to being a single parent of four, then crashing and burning in my life and coming back again, I've never lived according to other peoples' rules. And I try to inspire my children to know you can create your own wealth; in the entrepreneurial way of doing things there's no business as usual.

I'll leave you with one further thought. We all know how easy it is to waste all our time doing 'stuff'. And a lot of us do just that: stuff, stuff, stuff. But actually, if we spend our time on stuff we've not achieved anything, and if that happens every day then at the end of the quarter we've not achieved anything either. Then another year goes by, and we've not got as far on our journey as we would have liked.

So you've got to create a team in which every day counts. That's what a dream team is really about.

Chapter 7
Riding the entrepreneurial roller coaster

Chapter 7 **Riding the entrepreneurial roller coaster**

Congratulations. You've got to the point at which you're looking to the future. You have your team set up, your products, services and marketing are in place, and you're wondering where to go from here. How do you ensure your growing team continues to buy into your new culture, how do you learn from your successes and mistakes, and how do you look after yourself in all of this? And dare you enjoy the ride?

Here's some good news for you. You're not a machine! Nor am I, and nor is any entrepreneur who starts a brand new venture. We're all human – we get distracted, demotivated and interrupted, and that frustrates the heck out of us at times. I know it does me.

So how are you going to cope with this in your new journey? You have to figure out the strategies that work for you, and because we're all different, what's right for you won't necessarily be the same as it is for me. You've not got this far in your career without discovering what keeps you motivated, but that was in the days when you didn't have to think like an entrepreneur. Now you do.

What works for me

I'll start with me because, unsurprisingly, I'm the one I know the best! My hope is by seeing what helps me keep going, you'll get clues for what might work for you.

I'm very goal-orientated and love striving to achieve results, but I'm also easily distracted, especially with things I enjoy. I love a juicy problem; if I get a sniff of one in the office I'll drop everything to sort it out using my brilliant troubleshooting skills. But I have to ask myself: is this actually somebody else's problem to solve, and how is dealing with it any more important than doing my own work? So a lot of my focus throughout the day is based on keeping my attention on the important things and leaving my team to manage their own issues. To do this I find it helpful to have a morning routine and – this may surprise you – I make liberal use of the good old sticky note.

You'd laugh if you could see this but I have sticky notes all over my bedroom wall. As soon as I get up I do some stretches, then look at the notes which are reminding me to take care of three things: my health, my work and my spirit. Every day I try to do at least one thing that will increase my well-being, one thing that will take me closer to achieving my work goals and one thing that will lift my spirit.

My spiritual actions might involve me taking time to do something with my family or for my own development, or maybe I could just be kind to somebody that day. I know I'm blessed and I don't want to take what I have for granted, so my spiritual self is something I cherish.

As for my physical health, why is this so important to me? Because I know I'm only here once, so I have to take care of myself in order to be OK for everybody else. And my work is vital not just because it earns me money, but because it's a massive part of my life and a huge source of my enjoyment and sense of achievement.

What could you do to foster your health, work and spirit each day? What three things would make you feel more energetic, productive and content with yourself? They don't have to be momentous. How about swopping a car ride for a walk, avoiding the temptation to micro-manage your team and spending half an hour reading a favourite book tonight? These are all just examples; I'm sure you can come up with some great options that would work for you.

And one other thing, which will definitely surprise you: I don't have a desk. Because I know if I did there would be things on it for me to do, which would lead to me checking endless emails to find problems I could solve and get distracted by. I'd also end up sitting at it all day instead of getting out – in other words, talking to a computer instead of people. I bet the biggest thing on your desk right now is your computer or laptop, isn't it? You probably spend most of your time when you're at it tapping away on your keyboard, instead of talking on the phone or actually meeting someone face to face. You'll remember how important I said it was right at the beginning to avoid being a slave to your office, and there's no easier way to do this than not to have one in the first place!

So these are the ways I've developed to keep myself motivated, happy and fulfilled both in and outside work. I hope you find some ideas in here for you too.

Keeping inspired

Inspiration never comes on demand. Your greatest ideas will only arrive when you're least expecting them, so creating space in your schedule to let them in is vital. Hopefully by now you're making the effort to visit your employer companies more often, which is getting you out and about on a regular basis; this on its own will stimulate new ideas. But why not also block out an afternoon a month just to go for a walk? Being around people who are demanding things of you all the time can stifle your inspiration before it's even had a chance to arise.

How do you feel when you walk into your office? (I'm assuming you've still got one – it's probably a big leap to do away with it altogether like I have!) Do you feel your spirits lifting, or does your heart sink when you survey the drab walls and worn carpet tiles? You may not have the funds to do a full revamp, but a few pictures, a rug and a new lamp can make all the difference. Your physical environment is so important. We're human and we all need stimulation, variety and nice things around us to help us feel good throughout the day.

There are also other ways to encourage yourself to feel more positive by adding colour into your working environment. It might be that having different types of pens brightens you up and makes you feel more enthusiastic. I have a pad with three or four things mapped out in colour codes that I must do each day, which makes it really simple for me. No confusion, just focus.

Learning and developing in all areas

Of course, you're in the learning and development profession so you know all about continuous improvement. But it's easy to forget how much we can learn informally as well. If you think about it, you're constantly learning new things. When was the last time you took stock of what you've discovered over the past month? Do your colleagues ever do this? Could you find a way of sharing your learning and development, along with any exciting new things you've come across, in a mini-presentation with your team?

I'll give you an example from my own learning. I'm doing an MBA at the moment, and it's pretty time-consuming in terms of all the reading I have to do, but every now and again I come across a really fabulous nugget of information. In the leadership module recently we studied Daniel Goleman, which is all about emotional intelligence in the workplace, so I shared that with my own team on one of our dress-down Fridays. It went down a storm.

What about sharing some insights from a fantastic book you've read? Or how often do you go to a conference, but when you get back you're so busy catching up you forget to present the highlights to your team?

Another way of enhancing your own learning is to network with people who are different from you. I tend to mix with a lot of high achievers, so it's only when I spend time with people who have less of a can-do attitude that I realise how odd we entrepreneurs can be. You might find inspiration from meeting people with a different mindset to your own.

Although we still discover a lot of what we need from the professionals, we can constantly absorb knowledge just by being receptive and open. Learning happens by keeping a neutral mind and putting ourselves into situations that aren't necessarily comfortable or pre-planned. One of the best things I ever learned about was marketing; because everything's marketing, isn't it? We're all our own brand and have to work out how best to market ourselves. I got the dry facts about marketing through my Chartered Institute of Marketing qualification, but I actually learned the 'real' stuff when one of my sons did his marketing degree. He's very creative, so although I had more of an understanding of strategies and frameworks, he would throw ideas into the pot I would never have thought of. For me, that was learning.

Your equivalent to this could be going incognito into one of your classrooms for a day. That would teach you a lot about the culture in your college: how is lateness handled, what kind of clothes are considered acceptable and how does participation happen in class?

Learning comes from everywhere. It could be you discovering how to skateboard (OK that was a wild guess), or maybe you could develop knowledge about politics, or counselling skills or you could even do an MBA. You might already be going to a leadership club or a book club. It's not just about professional development, it's continuous learning in all areas. If you're not investing time in your own learning and sharing the knowledge, how can you expect the people within your team to do the same?

Broadening your world allows you to be inspired by all sorts of different places. If your learners will need to get a job at the end of their course and go through interview training, would you or your colleagues know what it feels like to be interviewed for one of those very jobs? Could you find out? So for instance, an interview for a newly qualified hairdresser might not just centre on the technical skills, it might also be based on how easy the candidate finds it to strike up a conversation with customers. Asking a hairdresser employer how they would judge an interviewee's soft skills might elicit the information that they look for them to be taking part in team activities outside work. So now you're learning the real information your young people need in order to get a job. Is that part of what you're delivering in your college?

I love putting myself in my clients' shoes. One of the ways I do this is by going out three or four times a year as a 'trainer' to deliver a course to our clients. They don't know it's me, nor do they really care, but it allows me to listen to feedback from them in an honest way. So if they mutter that something about our system is a bit convoluted, or 'why isn't the button for that there and not here?', I'm able to go back to my team and ask them to change it. Sometimes you have to make an active effort to put yourself out there in whatever way makes sense at the time. You certainly won't get all this from a formal training course.

Sometimes the higher up the career ladder we go, the less receptive we become to developing and changing. Our online Smart Leaders Club is yet another way of learning, this time from your peers. When you spend all day with your colleagues, who need you to appear confident and bulletproof, it can be a relief to let your guard down with others in the same boat as you.

Finding the time

'But wait a minute,' I hear you say. 'I've got a college to run. Where on earth am I going to find time for all this?'

To that I would answer: what are you currently spending your time doing? Is it on other peoples' 'stuff'? Or on things you enjoy, but (like my addiction to troubleshooting) aren't really the most important tasks right now? I have three or four key things on my to-do list every day, and I know if I don't do them I'm not going to get closer to my goals. For instance, today I need to create a contract for a new business partner and also give my sales team better marketing collateral to help them communicate our products more effectively. These are important mini-projects, not just 'stuff' I could do any day.

It's so easy to get dragged down into the nitty-gritty with our work, when we could have our minds on more important things. If you don't allow your team to manage the details you'll forever be juggling with multiple priorities, which means you'll never be free enough to learn and be inspired.

Moving on

I'll finish with this. Everything has a finite timescale, so your opportunity is to jump on it, make the most of it, and then know when it's time to move onto the next thing. For instance, as I mentioned earlier, three years ago we developed a version of our software that works offline for when people can't connect to Wi-Fi. Some of our clients recently asked us to redevelop it for a different purpose. But now that Wi-Fi is so much more readily available (by tethering from phones for instance), what was once in-novative and useful is now becoming obsolete. We have to move onto the next thing, not keep tinkering with the past.

I'm sure we've all been guilty of hanging onto something because it feels safe and comfortable, and there are hundreds of stories of businesses who've failed by doing just that. Think about the Blockbuster Videos of this world that have recently gone to the wall. Interestingly, Netflix started off with a similar business model to Blockbusters; the latter was store-based but Netflix sent videos and DVDs out by post. Then Netflix quickly realised they could deliver them more efficiently online. Who rents a physical DVD anymore?

You have to know when to withdraw your energy and time from one particular activity and get into something else. It can be scary, but oh so necessary.

This is the bit that brings me full circle. Because how do you know when it's the right time to move on? You have to be operating outside your own organisation to be aware of it. You need to be networking, spending time with employers, going to places you've not been to before and being open to suggestions and new learning. That's how you find out what your next move should be.

Conclusion

Conclusion

Now you've finished reading this book you may be thinking, *I had it all planned out. I was going to stay where I am for a while, maybe apply for a leadership position at another college, and then retire in 10 years' time. Now that's all changed.* And you're right. Because we don't know what the world is going to look like in 10 years' time, do we? Just think, a couple of years ago you would probably never have dreamed of entering the world of entrepreneurship, and now you're standing on the threshold of this new way of working.

And you can do it – you really can. One of the things I want to achieve with this book is to inspire you to believe that there are no limits for you. There's an infinite world of possibilities out there, and with your new-found knowledge and inspiration you can make the most of it for yourself, your college and your learners.

If you remember, first of all we looked at establishing your vision of where you want your college to be, and what kind of leader you'd love to become. Have you made inroads into this yet? I'm sure you've come up with some exciting dreams for the future.

Then we investigated various options for which strategic direction you go in, helped by identifying your potential clients' pain points so you can solve real problems, rather than the ones you think might exist. What ideas have you come up with so far – any you feel have good potential?

After that we went through how to launch your new product or service, both in terms of developing it to its full potential and marketing it effectively. I hope I've managed to convince you that this successful business model for launching is something you can apply successfully to your organisation.

And finally we unpicked the steps to recruiting and motivating your dream team, and how to sustain the momentum you've now built up, both for yourself and your colleagues. You can see success is more about what kind of attitude you have than what qualifications you've got.

You've also been on a journey of your own: from public sector leader to entrepreneurial visionary. It's quite a change, isn't it? Of course you still have your existing responsibilities, and you're not going to transform yourself overnight. Nor would you want to; it's your previous experience, tenacity and ability that's got you to where you are today. But you can see there's a different, dare I say more exciting, way of getting things done. A process that builds on what you're already great at and makes it even more effective; a path that leads to outcomes you can't even dream of yet.

Stirring stuff, isn't it? But underneath all this I'd love to leave you with this message: one of the hardest things in life is to learn to like and accept yourself. This book has challenged you in so many ways, so now's the time to come back and nurture yourself a bit. You've examined your strengths and weaknesses, your team make-up and your performance, and you've got yourself onto a dynamic trajectory. But you're still a person.

For me as the parent of four children, coming to a sense of acceptance of myself has been crucial, and is a massive achievement in its own right. It's not that I'm going to rest on my laurels and forget about learning anything new – far from it. But I have to know it's OK to be me. As my son says, 'Chill your beans, Mum.'

There is always, always going to be somebody who is better than you at certain things. You'll never be the fastest runner; you'll never be the best looking person; you'll never be the fittest or the brightest at everything. So given we're only here for a short space of time, let's get that sense of comfort from liking ourselves. Achieving success for your college is your goal, and the inner confidence you need to get there comes from self-acceptance.

With self-belief comes the willingness to take on new challenges, and fast. You don't have the luxury of waiting around to see what everyone else is doing. Start today. On my business journey with Smart Assessor I've learned that making quick, but considered, decisions is the secret of overcoming many a challenge. And I've enjoyed sharing my learnings with you.

Good luck, and I'm looking forward to hearing about what you get up to – just visit www.smartassessor.com and let me know how you're getting on.

About the author

About the author

Fiona Hudson-Kelly is the founder and CEO of Smart Assessor, the most innovative online assessing and learning
platform for students and apprentices in further education. Serving over 200 colleges and training providers,
along with over 125,000 learners, the system eliminates
paperwork and ensures colleges are audit ready every
day.

After founding the company in 2011, Fiona built it up
from zero to a £2m turnover, and has many more ambitious plans ahead. She's won numerous business awards,
including the 2013 Small Employer Apprentice of the
Year Award and 2016 Best Business Outstanding Female
Entrepreneur Award.

Now she's turning her hand to helping college leaders survive the challenges posed
by all the recent changes to further education. To further this aim, she's launched the
online Smart Leaders Club for college leaders who value peer support in making their
institutions more entrepreneurial. In it you'll find regular virtual events and a ready-
made community of senior, further education professionals who'll value your contribu-
tion and be willing to offer advice and support.

To find out more about the Smart Leaders Networking Club visit
www.smartassessor.com

You're also welcome to get in touch with Fiona for a chat about how technology can
help your college survive and thrive in the new economy. Just go to
www.smartassessor.com

The Smart Leaders Club

The Smart Leaders Club

It's lonely being a leader.

Scary too.

Often there is nobody you can confide in because you are supposed to be the brave strong person with all the answers. Yet when you do share your concerns, aspirations, ideas and failings everything seems so much brighter. Talking to other people like you, can give you back clarity and purpose.

Recently I was feeling jaded with the frustrations of trying to be superhuman; during my personal training session I shared this with my trainer James. He quickly inspired and encouraged me with his positive 'can do' attitude and the rest of my day was completely different and highly successful.

The Smart Leaders Club is a network for leaders in colleges. The purpose of the network is to create a safe, trusting environment where senior leaders can share the challenges they face in driving through change in their organisations to be more entrepreneurial. They can learn from each other and dare to try things that they wouldn't otherwise have had the confidence to try knowing that others have trodden this path too. It isnt a group just for women or for those from technology. I want it to be all inclusive for the senior leadership team, starting with the principals.

We meet face-to-face twice a year for an overnight residential coaching and net-working session with online discussion groups to establish a mentoring culture where you can buddy up to coach and support each other.

For more information on the Smart Leaders Club visit our website www.smartassessor.com

Notes